Come Live With Me and Be My Love

SACRED AND PROFANE LOVE, *Titian*

Come Live With Me and Be My Love

EDITED BY
Pamela Norris

A Bulfinch Press Book
LITTLE, BROWN AND COMPANY
Boston   New York   Toronto   London

For John

First edition

ISBN 0-8212-2044-6

Decorative illustrations by Nadine Wickenden
Designed by David Fordham
Please see page 120 for further acknowledgements.

A CIP catalogue record for this book
is available from the British Library
Library of Congress Catalog Card Number 93-70708

Published simultaneously in the United States of America by Bulfinch Press,
an imprint and trademark of Little, Brown and Company (Inc.),
in Great Britain by Little, Brown and Company (UK) Ltd,
and in Canada by Little, Brown & Company (Canada) Limited

PRINTED IN ITALY

Contents

Introduction

Come live with me and be my love,
And we will all the pleasures prove
That hills and valleys, dale and field,
And all the craggy mountains yield.

The famous invitation from Christopher Marlowe's passionate shepherd invokes a pastoral idyll where nature's pleasures are celebrated in poetry that is as apparently unsophisticated as its subject matter. During the reign of Elizabeth I (1558-1603), love among country folk was a popular theme of lyric poetry and featured in the sub-plots of the many plays that were written during the period. But the love tradition that was to inspire much of the most powerful and passionate poetry of the English Renaissance was courtly, and had evolved from the poignant songs of the French troubadours. It was a tradition that appealed to the young Henry VIII when he dressed himself up as Cœur Loyal and fought in the jousts to the pleasure and delighted anxiety of his lady Catherine of Aragon. The amorous intrigues – and perils – of Henry's court are eloquently revealed for the modern reader in the poetry of Sir Thomas Wyatt. This courtly tradition, with its suggestion of a complex network of emotional relationships, was to continue well into the seventeenth century, and indicates that writing and reading about the pains and pleasures of love was a favourite occupation for the well-educated.

The poems in this anthology span over 150 years, from the reign of Henry VIII to the Restoration of Charles II. They were written by a great variety of poets, from well-born courtiers such as Sir Philip Sidney and his friend Fulke Greville, to working poets such as Michael Drayton and William Shakespeare. The style and quality of the poems also varies as the rougher rhymes and rhythms of mediaeval verse became increasingly polished and the stock of poetic forms was increased by Italian and French models, culminating in the sophisticated elegance of the cavalier poets of the seventeenth century, Suckling and Robert Herrick.

The poets and their historical backgrounds might vary, as the 'golden age' of Elizabeth gave way to Stuart intransigence and the muddled years of the Civil War, but the themes of love poetry remained the same and are reflected in the five sections of this anthology. As Marlowe points out,

> It lies not in our power to love or hate,
> For will in us is over-ruled by fate

and 'LOVE HAS MANY FACES' celebrates the diversity of love and the beloved. In 'Sonnetto', Robert Greene reflects on love's contradictions, its lack of logic and its irresistible force. In 'Song', Ben Jonson imagines his ideal lover, a beautiful, witty, courtly lady, who understands the arts of flirtation and coquetry. Katherine Philips corrects this view in 'The Virgin' with a clear-sighted description of the qualities that really make a woman pleasing, but hers is an isolated voice. Herrick happily praises the erotic delights of rumpled clothing, and Spenser's mistress most closely resembles a garden in her fragrance and colourfulness. The mature woman is not neglected: Greville's sonnet 'The Nurse-Life Wheat' values the ripeness of the full-blown rose beyond the promise of the bud. The stately court poet, Sir Philip Sidney, introduces a more sober note. Not for him the empty gallantries of the stock court lover, the lavishly curled hair and the endless moaning about broken hearts. The sincerity of his feeling is proved by his silence: 'They love indeed who quake to say they love.'

Love's force is irresistible, but pain is its almost inevitable consequence. Not for nothing is love's messenger, winged Cupid, frequently depicted in the art of the period with arrow poised, ready to strike the heart of his unsuspecting victim. Thomas Lodge's 'Rosalynd's Madrigal' charmingly pictures Cupid's merry games, which are, alas, accompanied by the sting of his dart. Wyatt describes the familiar condition of wakefulness experienced by the unrequited lover:

> The clothes that on my bed do lie
> Always me think they lie awry

and Henry Howard contrasts the spontaneous fruitfulness of nature with his own loveless state.

The celebration of erotic love and the frank enjoyment of sexuality were subjects boldly tackled by the Elizabethan poets. John Donne's 'The Good-Morrow' links the age of seafaring and buccaneering exploration with the intimate discoveries of the bedroom. In 'The Sun Rising' he points out that, to lovers, the great events and personalities of the court are nothing:

> She is all states, and all Princes, I,
> Nothing else is.

However, conquest is still predominant in Donne's mind. Christopher Marlowe's vigorous translation of Ovid, 'Love in The Afternoon', is more preoccupied with sensual sport than the relationship between the individual and the state, and Spenser similarly conjures up a most alluring picture of erotic entanglement in 'The Bower of Bliss' – but here, the enjoyment of love is censured. The woman is seen as a wicked enchantress, a subtle spider who has used her beauty to dishonour a young nobleman.

The lover enjoys his love – and is quickly abandoned. If these poets are to be believed, the sixteenth-century woman was culpably fickle. Sir Thomas Wyatt was accused of having been intimate with the discredited Queen Anne Boleyn, and 'Whoso List to Hunt' describes the bafflement of a huntsman fruitlessly pursuing a deer that is the property of a wealthy ruler. In 'They Flee From Me', Wyatt bitterly describes a haunting encounter with a beautiful woman, who then casually abandons him for other, more attractive lovers. Donne's grim 'Song' claims that a ten-thousand-day pilgrimage would not reveal a constant woman, and even if it did,

> Yet she
> Will be
> False, ere I come, to two or three.

The anonymous 'Greensleeves' bemoans the expense of trying to please a faithless woman, and Ralegh's 'As You Came From The Holy Land' mourns the loss of love through the lover ageing:

> Love likes not the falling fruit
> From the withered tree.

As Marvell says in 'To His Coy Mistress', 'Time's winged chariot' has a tendency to rush on whether we will or no, and many of the poems in the final section urge the young woman to 'Gather ye rosebuds while ye may'. Youth and beauty are fleeting and must be enjoyed while still available. Fortunately, as Spenser points out in 'One Day I Wrote Her Name', poetry endures to immortalize the beloved, and age does not deter all lovers. Samuel Daniel pledges constancy to his love when she is old and faded, and Shakespeare's 'That Time of Year' quietly evokes the twilight time that precedes death. Love can endure even this. Sidney's answer to the riddle of mortality is to turn his mind to higher things: 'The Farewell to Worldly Love' praises the greater rewards of the spiritual life.

The poetic flowering of the English Renaissance was matched by a similar burgeoning in European art. While the English painters largely remained rooted in the mediaeval tradition until the seventeenth century, Italian art was struggling to liberate itself from the straitjacket of conventional forms and themes as early as the late 1300s. By the time of Henry VIII, artists such as Botticelli in Florence and Carpaccio in Venice had established new ways of depicting the world, introducing both technical innovation (in the use of colour and perspective, for example) and a revolution in what was deemed appropriate subject matter for the visual arts. In this, the artists frequently worked to a specific brief. In place of solemn and didactic religious themes, wealthy patrons increasingly wanted to adorn buildings with works that either celebrated their own pomp, splendour and civic status, or the beauty and variety of the human form and intellect. Favourite subjects were the love affairs of the gods and goddesses, such as Venus and Mars, or of classical heroes, such as Perseus' dramatic rescue of Andromeda. The female nude, typically Venus, the goddess of love, at her toilet or engaged in some kind of frolic with her son Cupid, or even the biblical Susanna, peered at in her bath by the old men, offered an opportunity for sumptuous works that delighted the eye, and allowed artist and viewer to enjoy the harmonies of the human body after the austerities of the Middle Ages. Portraits encouraged reflection on human psychology and enabled the wealthy to leave a record for grateful citizens, and formal narrative court painting, recording conquests or the meeting of the betrothed in a dynastic marriage, again provided an attractive means of publicly recognizing civic or court achievement.

The paintings that accompany the poems in *Come Live With Me and Be My Love* include works by a broad spectrum of European artists and equally reflect a delight in love and beauty, and also a profound sense of the evanescence of things. Titian's 'Bacchus and Ariadne' tells the story of the discovery by the god Bacchus of the mortal Ariadne, abandoned by Theseus on the island of Naxos after she had helped him escape from the Minotaur. Painted for a room in the castle of the Duke of Ferrara, the god seems to leap out of the canvas in a swirl of exuberant love for the young woman, his crimson cloak vivid against an unbelievably cerulean sky. He is accompanied, typically, by leopards and a riotous mob of revellers, and it is no wonder that Ariadne's first impulse is to flee.

Venus, love's supreme deity, was painted again and again. Botticelli imagines her birth, the goddess emerging in immaculate and mysterious beauty from a shell amidst the play of zephyrs and the light swell of the foaming spray, whilst Titian's 'Sacred and Profane Love' presents her in her twin aspects as celestial and earthly Venus. Perhaps surprisingly for the modern viewer, the clothed Venus is a metaphor for the material world, her rich attire symbolic of earthly vanities, while the naked Venus represents the innocence and purity of the heavenly state. The Spanish painter Velázquez' beautifully painted nude, 'The Toilet of Venus', was unusual in the stricter climate of post-Inquisition Spain. The focus of the painting is on the woman's pale and elegant body as she gazes in the mirror held by her winged son, the naughty Cupid of so many Elizabethan poems. By contrast, Giovanni Bellini's much earlier 'Young Woman with a Mirror', in which a young girl gazes at her reflection, with a country landscape in the background, is a tender evocation of unsophisticated self-regard.

Allegorical or secondary meanings were important to the Renaissance artist, pointing out a moral or reminding the viewer of the consequences of a particular act. The angled skull in Holbein's '"The Ambassadors"' is a reminder that death is an ever-present feature of life, even for the wealthy or successful, a theme popular with the love poets. Bronzino's 'An Allegory with Venus and Cupid' can be identified as a commentary on the transience and bitter fruits of love.

In England, the Queen, Gloriana, became increasingly a focus for allegorical interpretation, paradoxically incorporating both the characteristics of the goddess of love and of a virgin queen. The carefully staged 'Rainbow' portrait of Elizabeth I is replete with imagery that would have had special meanings for her courtiers. In her headdress she wears the crescent moon, symbol of the goddess Diana and thus associating the Queen with chastity, but also with the moon and therefore with the control of the seas and of rainfall, important for the maritime ruler of a small island dependent on good harvests. The serpent of wisdom appears richly jewelled on her arm, and her gown is embroidered with the eyes and ears of a watchful monarch ever alert to the good of her subjects, her ears permanently cocked for any whisper of treason. The central image of the rainbow, reminder of God's covenant with man, is the traditional symbol of peace.

Beautiful women, handsome and frequently melancholy young men, couples working or talking together or engaging in loveplay, the loves and rivalries of gods and goddesses, the meetings of kings with betrothed princesses, the enigmatic encounter between the merchant Arnolfini and his modest wife – but perhaps nothing in Renaissance art so appropriately reminds us of love and its pains as well as its pleasures as that first significant sexual encounter: Eve's irresistible offer of the fruit of the Tree of Knowledge to Adam in the Garden of Eden. Beautiful and poignant recreations of the earthly Paradise and its bitter loss recur throughout the Renaissance and remind us that then as now the enjoyment of love was not

unproblematic. But despite all, the impulse towards love persists, and in the pages of this anthology it can be enjoyed with as little pain and as much pleasure as the reader desires.

PAMELA NORRIS
LONDON, 1993

Love Has Many Faces

The Lover Ponders the Nature of Love and Celebrates the Beloved

PERSEUS FREEING ANDROMEDA, *Piero di Cosimo*

MERCURY INSTRUCTING CUPID BEFORE VENUS, *Antonio Allegri da Correggio*

Tell Me, Dearest, What is Love?

Tell me, dearest, what is love?
'Tis a lightning from above;
　'Tis an arrow, 'tis a fire,
　'Tis a boy they call Desire;
　　　'Tis a grave,
　　　Gapes to have
Those poor fools that long to prove.

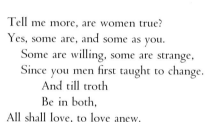

Tell me more, are women true?
Yes, some are, and some as you.
　Some are willing, some are strange,
　Since you men first taught to change.
　　　And till troth
　　　Be in both,
All shall love, to love anew.

Tell me more yet, can they grieve?
Yes, and sicken sore, but live,
　And be wise, and delay,
　When you men are as wise as they.
　　　Then I see,
　　　Faith will be,
Never till they both believe.

JOHN FLETCHER

Love at First Sight

Hero and Leander, ll. 167-176

It lies not in our power to love or hate,
For will in us is over-ruled by fate.
When two are stript long ere the course begin,
We wish that one should lose, the other win.
And one especially do we affect
Of two gold ingots like in each respect.
The reason no man knows; let it suffice,
What we behold is censured by our eyes.
Where both deliberate, the love is slight:
Who ever loved, that loved not at first sight?

CHRISTOPHER MARLOWE

LEDA, (after) *Leonardo da Vinci*

FLORA, *Carlo Cignani*

Coming to Kiss Her Lips

Coming to kiss her lips, (such grace I found),
   Me seemed I smelt a garden of sweet flowers:
   That dainty odours from them threw around
   For damsels fit to deck their lovers' bowers.
Her lips did smell like unto gillyflowers,
   Her ruddy cheeks like unto roses red,
   Her snowy brows like budded bellamours,
   Her lovely eyes like pinks but newly spread,
Her goodly bosom like a strawberry bed,
   Her neck like to a bunch of columbines,
   Her breast like lilies, ere their leaves be shed,
   Her nipples like young blossomed jessamines.
Such fragrant flowers do give most odorous smell,
   But her sweet odour did them all excel.

EDMUND SPENSER

Sonnetto

What thing is love? It is a power divine
That reigns in us, or else a wreakful law
That dooms our minds to beauty to incline:
It is a star, whose influence doth draw
    Our hearts to love, dissembling of his might
    Till he be master of our hearts and sight.

Love is a discord, and a strange divorce
Betwixt our sense and reason, by whose power,
As mad with reason, we admit that force
Which wit or labour never may devour:
    It is a will that brooketh no consent;
    It would refuse, yet never may repent.

Love's a desire, which for to wait a time,
Doth lose an age of years, and so doth pass,
As doth the shadow, severed from his prime,
Seeming as though it were, yet never was:
    Leaving behind nought but repentant thoughts
    Of days ill spent, for that which profits noughts.

It's now a peace, and then a sudden war;
A hope consumed before it is conceived;
At hand it fears, and menaceth afar;
And he that gains is most of all deceived:
    It is a secret hidden and not known,
    Which one may better feel than write upon.

ROBERT GREENE

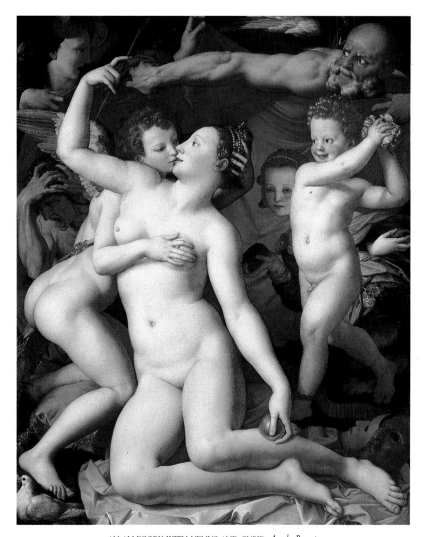

AN ALLEGORY WITH VENUS AND CUPID, *Agnolo Bronzino*

SELF-PORTRAIT WITH GLOVES, *Albrecht Dürer*

Because I Breathe Not Love

Because I breathe not love to every one,
  Nor do not use set colours for to wear,
  Nor nourish special locks of vowed hair,
Nor give each speech a full point of a groan,
The courtly nymphs, acquainted with the moan
  Of them, who in their lips love's standard bear:
  'What, he?' say they of me, 'now I dare swear,
He cannot love; no, no, let him alone.'
  And think so still, so Stella know my mind.
Profess indeed I do not Cupid's art;
But you, fair maids, at length this true shall find,
That his right badge is but worn in the heart;
  Dumb swans, not chattering pies, do lovers prove;
  They love indeed who quake to say they love.

SIR PHILIP SIDNEY

Song

If I freely may discover
What would please me in my lover:
   I would have her fair, and witty,
   Savouring more of court than city;
   A little proud, but full of pity;
   Light and humorous in her toying,
   Oft building hopes, and soon destroying,
   Long, but sweet in the enjoying,
Neither too easy, nor too hard:
All extremes I would have barred.

She should be allowed her passions,
So they were but used as fashions;
   Sometimes froward, and then frowning,
   Sometimes sickish, and then swowning,
   Every fit, with change, still crowning.
   Purely jealous, I would have her,
   Then only constant when I crave her;
   'Tis a virtue should not save her.
Thus, nor her delicates would cloy me,
Neither her peevishness annoy me.

BEN JONSON

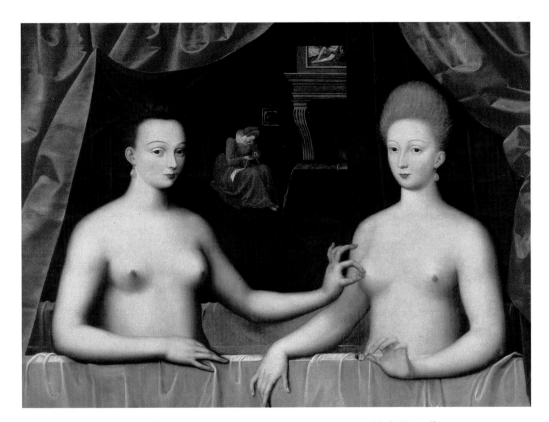

GABRIELLE D'ESTRÉES AND HER SISTER, THE DUCHESS OF VILLARS, *School of Fontainebleau*

'THE ARNOLFINI MARRIAGE', *Jan van Eyck*

The Virgin

The things that make a virgin please,
She that seeks, will find them these;
A beauty, not to art in debt,
Rather agreeable than great;
An eye, wherein at once do meet,
The beams of kindness, and of wit;
An undissembled innocence,
Apt not to give, nor take offence:
A conversation, at once, free
From passion, and from subtlety;
A face that's modest, yet serene,
A sober, and yet lively mien;
The virtue which does her adorn,
By honour guarded, not by scorn;
With such wise lowliness indued,
As never can be mean, or rude;
That prudent negligence enrich,
And time's her silence and her speech;
Whose equal mind, does always move,
Neither a foe, nor slave to love;
And whose religion's strong and plain,
Not superstitious, nor profane.

KATHERINE PHILIPS

On His Mistress,
The Queen of Bohemia

You meaner beauties of the night,
    That poorly satisfy our eyes
More by your number than your light,
    You common people of the skies;
    What are you when the moon shall rise?

You curious chanters of the wood,
    That warble forth Dame Nature's lays,
Thinking your passions understood
    By your weak accents; what's your praise
    When Philomel her voice shall raise?

You violets that first appear,
    By your pure purple mantles known
Like the proud virgins of the year,
    As if the spring were all your own;
    What are you when the rose is blown?

So, when my mistress shall be seen
    In form and beauty of her mind,
By virtue first, then choice, a Queen,
    Tell me if she were not designed
    The eclipse and glory of her kind?

SIR HENRY WOTTON

NON·SINE·SOLE
IRIS.

THE 'RAINBOW' PORTRAIT OF QUEEN ELIZABETH I, *Isaac Oliver* (?)

Delight in Disorder

A sweet disorder in the dress
Kindles in clothes a wantonness:
A lawn about the shoulders thrown
Into a fine distraction;
An erring lace, which here and there
Enthrals the crimson stomacher;
A cuff neglectful, and thereby
Ribbands to flow confusedly;
A winning wave (deserving note)
In the tempestuous petticoat;
A careless shoestring, in whose tie
I see a wild civility;
Do more bewitch me, than when art
Is too precise in every part.

ROBERT HERRICK

PASTORAL CONCERT, *Titian*

PORTRAIT OF A LADY, *Francesco Urbertini Verdi*

The Nurse-Life Wheat

The nurse-life wheat within his green husk growing,
Flatters our hope, and tickles our desire,
Nature's true riches in sweet beauties showing,
Which set all hearts, with labour's love, on fire.

No less fair is the wheat when golden ear,
Shows unto hope the joys of near enjoying:
Fair and sweet is the bud, more sweet and fair
The rose, which proves that time is not destroying.

Cælica, your youth, the morning of delight,
Enamelled o'er with beauties white and red,
All sense and thoughts did to belief invite,
That love and glory there are brought to bed;
    And your ripe years love none – he goes no higher –
    Turns all the spirits of man into desire.

FULKE GREVILLE, LORD BROOKE

love none = love's noon

The Pain of Love

THE LOVER SUFFERS FROM CUPID'S CARELESS DART

PRIMAVERA (detail), *Sandro Botticelli*

PORTRAIT OF A YOUNG MAN, *Isaac Oliver*

In Youth is Pleasure

In a herber green, asleep where as I lay,
The birds sang sweet in the mids of the day;
I dreamed fast of mirth and play.
  In youth is pleasure, in youth is pleasure.

Me thought as I walked still to and fro,
And from her company I could not go,
But when I waked it was not so.
  In youth is pleasure, in youth is pleasure.

Therefore my heart is surely pight
Of her alone to have a sight,
Which is my joy and heart's delight.
  In youth is pleasure, in youth is pleasure.

ROBERT WEAVER

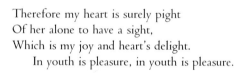

pight = fixed

Rosalynd's Madrigal

Love in my bosom like a bee
    Doth suck his sweet;
Now with his wings he plays with me,
    Now with his feet.
Within mine eyes he makes his nest,
His bed amidst my tender breast,
My kisses are his daily feast,
And yet he robs me of my rest.
    Ah, wanton, will ye?

And if I sleep, then percheth he
    With pretty flight,
And makes his pillow of my knee
    The livelong night.
Strike I my lute, he tunes the string;
He music plays, if so I sing;
He lends me every lovely thing;
Yet cruel he my heart doth sting.
    Whist, wanton, still ye!

Else I with roses every day
    Will whip you hence,
And bind you when you long to play,
    For your offence.
I'll shut my eyes to keep you in,
I'll make you fast it for your sin,
I'll count your power not worth a pin.
Alas, what hereby shall I win,
    If he gainsay me?

What if I beat the wanton boy
    With many a rod?
He will repay me with annoy,
    Because a god.
Then sit thou safely on my knee,
And let thy bower my bosom be,
Lurk in mine eyes, I like of thee,
O Cupid, so thou pity me,
    Spare not, but play thee.

THOMAS LODGE

CUPID COMPLAINING TO VENUS, *Lucas Cranach the Elder*

Of The Pains and Sorrows Caused by Love

What meaneth this? When I lie alone,
I toss, I turn, I sigh, I groan;
My bed me seems as hard as stone:
    What means this?

I sigh, I plain continually;
The clothes that on my bed do lie
Always me think they lie awry:
    What means this?

In slumbers oft for fear I quake;
For heat and cold I burn and shake;
For lack of sleep my head doth ache:
    What means this?

A-mornings then when I do rise,
I turn unto my wonted guise,
All day after muse and devise:
    What means this?

And if perchance by me there pass
She unto whom I sue for grace,
The cold blood forsaketh my face:
    What means this?

But if I sit near her by,
With loud voice my heart doth cry,
And yet my mouth is dumb and dry:
    What means this?

To ask for help no heart I have,
My tongue doth fail what I should crave,
Yet inwardly I rage and rave:
    What means this?

Thus have I passed many a year,
And many a day, though nought appear;
But most of that that most I fear:
    What means this?

SIR THOMAS WYATT

PORTRAIT OF A YOUNG MAN, *Moretto da Brescia*

THE MONTH OF APRIL (detail), *Francesco del Cossa*

The Soote Season

The soote season, that bud and bloom forth brings,
  With green hath clad the hill and eke the vale;
The nightingale with feathers new she sings,
  The turtle to her make hath told her tale.
Summer is come, for every spray now springs;
  The hart hath hung his old head on the pale,
The buck in brake his winter coat he flings,
  The fishes float with new repaired scale,
The adder all her slough away she slings.
  The swift swallow pursueth the flies small,
The busy bee her honey now she mings,
  Winter is worn that was the flowers' bale.
And thus I see among these pleasant things
Each care decays; and yet my sorrow springs.

Henry Howard, Earl of Surrey

soote = sweet

Loving in Truth

Loving in truth, and fain in verse my love to show,
    That she (dear she) might take some pleasure of my pain:
    Pleasure might cause her read, reading might make her know,
    Knowledge might pity win, and pity grace obtain;
I sought fit words to paint the blackest face of woe,
    Studying inventions fine, her wits to entertain,
    Oft turning others' leaves, to see if thence would flow
    Some fresh and fruitful showers upon my sun-burned brain.
But words came halting forth, wanting invention's stay;
    Invention, nature's child, fled step-dame study's blows:
    And others' feet still seemed but strangers in my way.
Thus great with child to speak, and helpless in my throes,
    Biting my truant pen, beating my self for spite:
    'Fool,' said my muse to me, 'look in thy heart and write.'

SIR PHILIP SIDNEY

PORTRAIT OF AN UNKNOWN MAN, *Hans Memling*

THE YOUNG BACCHUS, *Michelangelo Merisi da Caravaggio*

Love in a Humour

Love in a humour played the prodigal,
And bade my senses to a solemn feast,
Yet more to grace the company withal,
Invites my heart to be the chiefest guest;
No other drink would serve this glutton's turn
But precious tears distilling from mine eyne,
Which with my sighs this epicure doth burn,
Quaffing carouses in this costly wine,
Where, in his cups o'ercome with foul excess,
Begins to play a swaggering ruffian's part,
And at the banquet, in his drunkenness,
Slew my dear friend, his kind and truest heart.
    A gentle warning, friends, thus may you see,
    What 'tis to keep a drunkard company.

MICHAEL DRAYTON

The Expense of Spirit

The expense of spirit in a waste of shame
Is lust in action, and till action, lust
Is perjured, murderous, bloody, full of blame,
Savage, extreme, rude, cruel, not to trust,
Enjoyed no sooner but despised straight,
Past reason hunted, and no sooner had,
Past reason hated as a swallowed bait
On purpose laid to make the taker mad;
Mad in pursuit and in possession so,
Had, having, and in quest to have, extreme,
A bliss in proof, and proved, a very woe,
Before, a joy proposed, behind, a dream.
    All this the world well knows, yet none knows well
    To shun the heaven that leads men to this hell.

WILLIAM SHAKESPEARE

THE RAPE OF PROSERPINE, *Niccolò dell'Abate*

To Lucasta, Going to The Wars

Tell me not, sweet, I am unkind,
  That from the nunnery
Of thy chaste breast, and quiet mind,
  To war and arms I fly.

True, a new mistress now I chase,
  The first foe in the field;
And with a stronger faith embrace
  A sword, a horse, a shield.

Yet this inconstancy is such
  As you too shall adore;
I could not love thee, dear, so much,
  Loved I not honour more.

Richard Lovelace

PORTRAIT OF A CAVALIER, *Vittore Carpaccio*

ARIADNE ABANDONED, *Gerolamo del Pacchia*

O Happy Dames

O happy dames, that may embrace
   The fruit of your delight,
Help to bewail the woeful case
   And eke the heavy plight
Of me, that wonted to rejoice
The fortune of my pleasant choice;
Good ladies, help to fill my mourning voice.

In ship, freight with rememberance
   Of thoughts and pleasures past,
He sails that hath in governance
   My life while it will last;
With scalding sighs, for lack of gale,
Furthering his hope, that is his sail,
Toward me, the sweet port of his avail.

Alas, how oft in dreams I see
   Those eyes that were my food;
Which sometime so delighted me,
   That yet they do me good;
Wherewith I wake with his return,
Whose absent flame did make me burn:
But when I find the lack, Lord, how I mourn!

When other lovers in arms across
   Rejoice their chief delight,
Drowned in tears, to mourn my loss
   I stand the bitter night
In my window, where I may see
Before the winds how the clouds flee.
Lo, what a mariner love hath made me!

And in green waves when the salt flood
   Doth rise by rage of wind,
A thousand fancies in that mood
   Assail my restless mind.
Alas, now drencheth my sweet foe,
That with the spoil of my heart did go,
And left me; but, alas, why did he so?

And when the seas wax calm again
   To chase from me annoy,
My doubtful hope doth cause me plain;
   So dread cuts off my joy.
Thus is my wealth mingled with woe,
And of each thought a doubt doth grow;
'Now he comes! Will he come? Alas, no, no!'

HENRY HOWARD, EARL OF SURREY

Love's Joys

The Lover Expresses Passionate Delight and Gratitude on Enjoying the Beloved

THE MEETING OF ST URSULA WITH HER BETROTHED (detail),
Vittore Carpaccio

Love in The Afternoon

In summer's heat, and mid-time of the day,
To rest my limbs, upon a bed I lay.
One window shut, the other open stood,
Which gave such light as twinkles in a wood,
Like twilight glimpse at setting of the sun,
Or night being past, and yet not day begun;
Such light to shamefaced maidens must be
       shown
Where they may sport, and seem to be unknown.
Then came Corinna in a long loose gown,
Her white neck hid with tresses hanging down,
Resembling fair Semiramis going to bed,
Or Läis of a thousand lovers sped.
I snatched her gown; being thin, the harm was
       small;

Yet strived she to be covered therewithal;
And striving thus, as one that would be cast,
Betrayed herself, and yielded at the last.
Stark naked as she stood before mine eye,
Not one wen in her body could I spy.
What arms and shoulders did I touch and see,
How apt her breasts were to be pressed by me!
How smooth a belly under her waist saw I,
How large a leg, and what a lusty thigh!
To leave the rest, all liked me passing well:
I clinged her naked body; down she fell.
Judge you the rest: being tired, she bade me kiss.
Jove send me more such afternoons as this.

CHRISTOPHER MARLOWE

THE VENUS OF URBINO, *Titian*

Pack, Clouds, Away

Pack, clouds, away, and welcome day,
　　With night we banish sorrow;
Sweet air blow soft, mount larks aloft,
　　To give my love good-morrow!
Wings from the wind to please her mind,
　　Notes from the lark I'll borrow;
Bird prune thy wing, nightingale sing,
　　To give my love good-morrow;
　　　　To give my love good-morrow
　　　　Notes from them both I'll borrow.

Wake from thy nest, robin-red-breast,
　　Sing birds in every furrow;
And from each hill, let music shrill,
　　Give my fair love good-morrow!
Blackbird and thrush in every bush,
　　Stare, linnet, and cock-sparrow!
You pretty elves, amongst yourselves
　　Sing my fair love good-morrow;
　　　　To give my love good-morrow
　　　　Sing birds in every furrow!

THOMAS HEYWOOD

THE CONTEST BETWEEN MARSYAS AND APOLLO, *Pietro Vanucci Perugino*

THE MONEYLENDER AND HIS WIFE, *Quentin Massys*

My True Love Hath My Heart

My true love hath my heart, and I have his,
By just exchange one for the other given.
I hold his dear, and mine he cannot miss:
There never was a better bargain driven.
His heart in me keeps me and him in one;
My heart in him his thoughts and senses guides;
He loves my heart for once it was his own;
I cherish his because in me it bides.
His heart his wound received from my sight;
My heart was wounded with his wounded heart;
For as from me on him his hurt did light,
So still, me thought, in me his hurt did smart;
    Both equal hurt, in this change sought our bliss:
    My true love hath my heart, and I have his.

Sir Philip Sidney

The Sun Rising

Busy old fool, unruly sun,
　　Why dost thou thus,
Through windows, and through curtains call on
　　　　　　　　us?
Must to thy motions lovers' seasons run?
　　　　Saucy pedantic wretch, go chide
　　　　Late schoolboys, and sour prentices,
　　Go tell court-huntsmen that the King will
　　　　　　　　ride,
　　Call country ants to harvest offices;
Love, all alike, no season knows nor clime,
Nor hours, days, months, which are the rags of
　　　　　　　　time.

　　　Thy beams so reverend, and strong,
　　　　Dost thou not think
I could eclipse and cloud them with a wink,
But that I would not lose her sight so long?
　　　　If her eyes have not blinded thine,
　　　　Look, and tomorrow late, tell me
　　Whether both the Indias of spice and mine
　　Be where thou left them, or lie here with me.
Ask for those Kings whom thou saw'st yesterday,
And thou shalt hear, All here in one bed lay.

　　　She is all states, and all Princes, I,
　　　　Nothing else is.
Princes do but play us; compared to this,
All honour's mimic; all wealth alchemy.
　　　　Thou sun art half as happy as we,
　　　　In that the world's contracted thus.
　　Thine age asks ease, and since thy duties be
　　To warm the world, that's done in warming
　　　　　　　　us.
Shine here to us, and thou art everywhere;
This bed thy centre is, these walls, thy sphere.

JOHN DONNE

THE MEETING OF FREDERICK III AND ELEANOR OF ARAGON (detail), *Bernardino Betti, Il Pinturicchio*

THE THREE AGES OF MAN (detail), *Titian*

The Passionate Shepherd to His Love

Come live with me and be my love,
And we will all the pleasures prove
That hills and valleys, dale and field,
And all the craggy mountains yield.

There will we sit upon the rocks
And see the shepherds feed their flocks,
By shallow rivers, to whose falls
Melodious birds sing madrigals.

There will I make thee beds of roses
And a thousand fragrant posies,
A cap of flowers, and a kirtle
Embroidered all with leaves of myrtle.

A gown made of the finest wool,
Which from our pretty lambs we pull,
Fair lined slippers for the cold,
With buckles of the purest gold.

A belt of straw and ivy buds
With coral clasps and amber studs:
And if these pleasures may thee move,
Come live with me and be my love.

The shepherd swains shall dance and sing
For thy delight each May-morning:
If these delights thy mind may move,
Then live with me and be my love.

CHRISTOPHER MARLOWE

The Good-Morrow

I wonder by my troth, what thou and I
Did, till we loved? Were we not weaned till then,
But sucked on country pleasures childishly?
Or snorted we in the seven sleepers' den?
'Twas so; but this, all pleasures fancies be:
If ever any beauty I did see,
Which I desired, and got, 'twas but a dream of thee.

And now good-morrow to our waking souls,
Which watch not one another out of fear;
For love all love of other sights controls,
And makes one little room an everywhere.
Let sea-discoverers to new worlds have gone,
Let maps to other, worlds on worlds have shown,
Let us possess one world; each hath one, and is one.

My face in thine eye, thine in mine appears,
And true plain hearts do in the faces rest;
Where can we find two fitter hemispheres
Without sharp north, without declining west?
Whatever dies, was not mixed equally;
If our two loves be one, both thou and I
Love just alike in all, none of these loves can die.

JOHN DONNE

A MAN AND A WOMAN AT A CASEMENT, *Fra Filippo Lippi*

THE HUNT OF CHARLES V (detail), *Lucas Cranach the Elder*

Like as a Huntsman

Like as a huntsman after weary chase,
  Seeing the game from him escaped away,
  Sits down to rest him in some shady place,
  With panting hounds beguiled of their prey:
So after long pursuit and vain assay,
  When I all weary had the chase forsook,
  The gentle deer returned the self-same way,
  Thinking to quench her thirst at the next brook.
There she, beholding me with milder look,
  Sought not to fly, but fearless still did bide:
  Till I in hand her yet half trembling took,
  And with her own good will her firmly tied.
Strange thing, me seemed, to see a beast so wild
  So goodly won, with her own will beguiled.

EDMUND SPENSER

The World, That All Contains

The world, that all contains, is ever moving;
　　The stars within their spheres for ever turned;
Nature, the queen of change, to change is loving,
　　And form to matter new is still adjourned.
Fortune, our fancy-god, to vary liketh;
　　Place is not bound to things within it placed;
The present time upon time passed striketh;
　　With Phoebus' wandering course the earth is graced.
The air still moves, and by its moving cleareth;
　　The fire up ascends and planets feedeth;
The water passeth on and all lets weareth;
　　The earth stands still, yet change of changes breedeth.
Her plants, which summer ripens, in winter fade;
　　Each creature in unconstant mother lieth;
Man made of earth, and for whom earth is made,
　　Still dying lives, and living ever dieth.
　　　　Only, like fate, sweet Myra never varies,
　　　　Yet in her eyes the doom of all change carries.

FULKE GREVILLE, LORD BROOKE

THE RAPE OF EUROPA, *Francesco Albani*

VENUS AND MARS, *Sandro Botticelli*

The Bower of Bliss

From *The Faerie Queene*, Book 2, Canto xii

Upon a bed of roses she was laid,
　　As faint through heat, or dight to pleasant sin,
　　And was arrayed, or rather disarrayed,
　　All in a veil of silk and silver thin,
　　That hid no whit her alabaster skin,
　　But rather showed more white, if more might be:
　　More subtle web Arachne cannot spin,
　　Nor the fine nets, which oft we woven see
Of scorched dew, do not in th'air more lightly
　　　　　　　　　　　flee.

Her snowy breast was bare to ready spoil
　　Of hungry eyes, which n'ote therewith be
　　　　　　　　　　filled,
　　And yet, through languor of her late sweet
　　　　　　　　　　toil,
　　Few drops, more clear than nectar, forth
　　　　　　　　　　distilled,
　　That like pure Orient pearls adown it trilled,
　　And her fair eyes, sweet smiling in delight,
　　Moistened their fiery beams, with which she
　　　　　　　　　　thrilled
　　Frail hearts, yet quenched not; like starry light
Which, sparkling on the silent waves, does seem
　　　　　　　　　　more bright.

The young man sleeping by her seemed to be
　　Some goodly swain of honourable place,
　　That certes it great pity was to see
　　Him his nobility so foul deface;
　　A sweet regard and amiable grace,
　　Mixed with manly sternness, did appear
　　Yet sleeping, in his well-proportioned face,
　　And on his tender lips the downy hair
Did now but freshly spring, and silken blossoms
　　　　　　　　　　bear.

His warlike arms, the idle instruments
　　Of sleeping praise, were hung upon a tree,
　　And his brave shield, full of old monuments,
　　Was foully razed, that none the signs might
　　　　　　　　　　see;
　　Nor for them, nor for honour cared he,
　　Nor ought that did to his advancement tend,
　　But in lewd loves, and wasteful luxury,
　　His days, his goods, his body, he did spend:
O horrible enchantment, that him so did blend.

EDMUND SPENSER

n'ote = could not　　　blend = blind

The Lover Abandoned

The Lover Expresses Grief and Bitterness at the Fickleness of the Beloved

THE ANDRIANS, *Titian*

Whoso List to Hunt

Whoso list to hunt, I know where is an hind,
   But as for me, alas, I may no more.
   The vain travail hath wearied me so sore,
I am of them that furthest come behind.
Yet may I by no means my wearied mind
   Draw from the deer, but as she fleeth afore
   Fainting I follow. I leave off therefore
Since in a net I seek to hold the wind.
Who list her hunt, I put him out of doubt,
   As well as I may spend his time in vain.
   And graven with diamonds in letters plain
There is written her fair neck round about:
   '*Noli me tangere* for Caesar's I am,
   And wild for to hold though I seem tame.'

SIR THOMAS WYATT

DIANA THE HUNTER, *Orazio Gentileschi*

A BLONDE WOMAN, *Palma Vecchio*

A New Courtly Sonnet of
The Lady Greensleeves

Greensleeves was all my joy,
  Greensleeves was my delight;
Greensleeves was my heart of gold,
  And who but Lady Greensleeves.

Alas, my love, you do me wrong
  To cast me off discourteously;
And I have loved you so long,
  Delighting in your company.

I have been ready at your hand,
  To grant whatever you would crave;
I have both waged life and land,
  Your love and good will for to have.

Thy gown was of the grassy green,
  Thy sleeves of satin hanging by,
Which made thee be our harvest queen,
  And yet thou wouldst not love me.

My gayest gelding I thee gave,
  To ride wherever liked thee;
No lady ever was so brave,
  And yet thou wouldst not love me.

For every morning when thou rose,
  I sent thee dainties orderly,
To cheer thy stomach from all woes,
  And yet thou wouldst not love me.

And who did pay for all this gear
  That thou didst spend when pleased thee?
Even I that am rejected here,
  And thou disdainst to love me.

Well, I will pray to God on high,
  That thou my constancy mayst see,
And that yet once before I die
  Thou wilt vouchsafe to love me.

Greensleeves, now farewell! adieu!
  God I pray to prosper thee;
For I am still thy lover true,
  Come once again and love me.
    Greensleeves was all my joy,
      Greensleeves was my delight;
    Greensleeves was my heart of gold,
      And who but Lady Greensleeves.

(Abridged)   ANONYMOUS

They Flee From Me

They flee from me that sometime did me seek
With naked foot stalking within my chamber.
Once have I seen them gentle, tame, and meek
That now are wild, and do not once remember
That sometime they have put themselves in danger
To take bread at my hand; and now they range
Busily seeking in continual change.

Thanked be fortune it hath been otherwise
Twenty times better, but once especial,
In thin array after a pleasant guise,
When her loose gown did from her shoulders fall
And she me caught in her arms long and small,
And therewithal so sweetly did me kiss
And softly said, 'Dear heart, how like you this?'

It was no dream: for I lay broad awaking.
But all is turned now through my gentleness
Into a bitter fashion of forsaking.
And I have leave to go of her goodness
And she also to use newfangleness.
But, since that I unkindly so am served,
How like you this, what hath she now deserved?

SIR THOMAS WYATT

BACCHUS AND ARIADNE, *Titian*

THE MAGDALENE, *Michelangelo Merisi da Caravaggio*

The Sun is Set

The sun is set, and masked night
Vails heaven's fair eyes.
Ah, what trust is there to a light
That so swift flies.

A new world doth his flames enjoy
New hearts rejoice.
In other eyes is now his joy
In other choice.

ROBERT SIDNEY, EARL OF LEICESTER

Song

Go and catch a falling star,
   Get with child a mandrake root,
Tell me where all past years are,
   Or who cleft the devil's foot,
Teach me to hear mermaids singing,
Or to keep off envy's stinging,
         And find
         What wind
Serves to advance an honest mind.

If thou beest born to strange sights,
   Things invisible to see,
Ride ten thousand days and nights,
   Till age snow white hairs on thee;
Thou, when thou returnest, wilt tell me
All strange wonders that befell thee,
         And swear
         No where
Lives a woman true, and fair.

If you find'st one, let me know,
   Such a pilgrimage were sweet;
Yet do not, I would not go,
   Though at next door we might meet;
Though she were true when you met her,
And last, till you write your letter,
         Yet she
         Will be
False, ere I come, to two or three.

JOHN DONNE

THE PEARL FISHERS, *Alessandro Allori*

SUSANNA AT HER BATH, *Palma il Giovane*

As You Came From The Holy Land

As you came from the holy land
   Of Walsingham,
Met you not with my true love
   By the way as you came?

How shall I know your true love,
   That have met many one
As I went to the holy land,
   That have come, that have gone?

She is neither white nor brown,
   But as the heavens fair,
There is none hath a form so divine
   In the earth or the air.

Such an one did I meet, good sir,
   Such an angelic face,
Who like a queen, like a nymph, did appear
   By her gait, by her grace.

She hath left me here all alone,
   All alone as unknown,
Who sometimes did me lead with herself,
   And loved me as her own.

What's the cause that she leaves you alone
   And a new way doth take,
Who loved you once as her own
   And her joy did you make?

I have loved her all my youth,
   But now old, as you see;
Love likes not the falling fruit
   From the withered tree.

Know that Love is a careless child,
   And forgets promise past;
He is blind, he is deaf when he list,
   And in faith never fast.

His desire is a dureless content
   And a trustless joy;
He is won with a world of despair
   And is lost with a toy.

But true love is a durable fire
   In the mind ever burning;
Never sick, never old, never dead,
   From itself never turning.

(Abridged)   SIR WALTER RALEGH

Song

Why so pale and wan, fond lover?
    Prithee, why so pale?
Will, when looking well can't move her,
    Looking ill prevail?
    Prithee, why so pale?

Why so dull and mute, young sinner?
    Prithee, why so mute?
Will, when speaking well can't win her,
    Saying nothing do't?
    Prithee, why so mute?

Quit, quit, for shame, this will not move,
    This cannot take her;
If of herself she will not love,
    Nothing can make her:
    The devil take her.

SIR JOHN SUCKLING

SERVANTS WITH A HORSE AND DOGS (detail), *Andrea Mantegna*

PORTRAIT OF A LADY, *Lorenzo Lotto*

A Renunciation

If women could be fair, and yet not fond,
    Or that their love were firm, not fickle still,
I would not marvel that they make men bond
    By service long to purchase their good will;
But when I see how frail those creatures are,
I muse that men forget themselves so far.

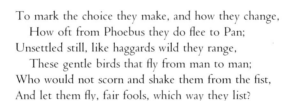

To mark the choice they make, and how they change,
    How oft from Phoebus they do flee to Pan;
Unsettled still, like haggards wild they range,
    These gentle birds that fly from man to man;
Who would not scorn and shake them from the fist,
And let them fly, fair fools, which way they list?

Yet for disport we fawn and flatter both,
    To pass the time when nothing else can please,
And train them to our lure with subtle oath,
    Till, weary of their wiles, ourselves we ease;
And then we say when we their fancy try,
To play with fools, O what a fool was I!

EDWARD DE VERE, EARL OF OXFORD

Farewell, False Love

Farewell, false love, the oracle of lies,
   A mortal foe, and enemy to rest,
An envious boy, from whom all cares arise,
   A bastard vile, a beast with rage possessed,
     A way of error, a temple full of treason,
     In all effects contrary unto reason.

A poisoned serpent covered all with flowers,
   Mother of sighs, and murderer of repose,
A sea of sorrows from whence are drawn such
              showers,
   As moisture lend, to every grief that grows,
     A school of guile, a net of deep deceit,
     A gilded hook that holds a poisoned bait.

A fortress foiled, which reason did defend,
   A siren song, a fever of the mind,
A maze wherein affection finds no end,
   A raging cloud that runs before the wind,
     A substance like the shadow of the sun,
     A goal of grief for which the wisest run.

A quenchless fire, a nurse of trembling fear,
   A path that leads to peril and mishap,
A true retreat of sorrow and despair,
   An idle boy that sleeps in pleasure's lap,
     A deep mistrust of that which certain seems,
     A hope of that which reason doubtful deems.

SIR WALTER RALEGH

ADAM, *Lucas Cranach the Elder*

EVE, *Lucas Cranach the Elder*

Love and Time

THE LOVER REMINDS THE
BELOVED THAT YOUTH AND
BEAUTY DO NOT LAST; BUT
TIME DOES OFFER SOLACE

THE BIRTH OF VENUS, *Sandro Botticelli*

Song

Go lovely rose,
Tell her that wastes her time and me,
That now she knows,
When I resemble her to thee,
How sweet and fair she seems to be.

Tell her that's young,
And shuns to have her graces spied,
That hadst thou sprung
In deserts where no men abide,
Thou must have uncommended died.

Small is the worth
Of beauty from the light retired;
Bid her come forth,
Suffer her self to be desired,
And not blush so to be admired.

Then die, that she
The common fate of all things rare
May read in thee,
How small a part of time they share,
That are so wondrous sweet and fair.

EDMUND WALLER

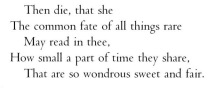

THE TOILET OF VENUS, *Diego Velázquez*

Ö Mistress Mine

O mistress mine, where are you roaming?
O stay and hear! your true-love's coming
    That can sing both high and low;
Trip no further, pretty sweeting,
Journeys end in lovers' meeting –
    Every wise man's son doth know.

What is love? 'tis not hereafter;
Present mirth hath present laughter;
    What's to come is still unsure:
In delay there lies no plenty –
Then come kiss me, sweet-and-twenty,
    Youth's a stuff will not endure.

WILLIAM SHAKESPEARE

PORTRAIT OF A LADY, *Lucas Cranach the Elder*

VENUS AND MARS, *Paolo Veronese*

To The Virgins, To Make Much of Time

Gather ye rosebuds while ye may,
   Old Time is still a-flying:
And this same flower that smiles today
   Tomorrow will be dying.

The glorious lamp of heaven, the sun,
   The higher he's a-getting,
The sooner will his race be run,
   And nearer he's to setting.

That age is best which is the first,
   When youth and blood are warmer;
But being spent, the worse, and worst
   Times still succeed the former.

Then be not coy, but use your time,
   And while ye may, go marry:
For having lost but once your prime,
   You may for ever tarry.

ROBERT HERRICK

To His Love

Shall I compare thee to a summer's day?
　　Thou art more lovely and more temperate:
Rough winds do shake the darling buds of May,
　　And summer's lease hath all too short a date:
Sometime too hot the eye of heaven shines,
　　And often is his gold complexion dimmed:
And every fair from fair sometime declines,
　　By chance, or nature's changing course, untrimmed.
But thy eternal summer shall not fade
　　Nor lose possession of that fair thou owest;
Nor shall death brag thou wanderest in his shade,
　　When in eternal lines to time thou growest.
　　　　So long as men can breathe, or eyes can see,
　　　　So long lives this, and this gives life to thee.

WILLIAM SHAKESPEARE

PORTRAIT OF A LADY IN YELLOW, *Alesso Baldovinetti*

To His Coy Mistress

Had we but world enough, and time,
This coyness, lady, were no crime.
We would sit down and think which way
To walk and pass our long love's day.
Thou by the Indian Ganges side
Should'st rubies find: I by the tide
Of Humber would complain. I would
Love you ten years before the flood:
And you should if you please refuse
Till the conversion of the Jews.
My vegetable love should grow
Vaster than empires, and more slow.
An hundred years should go to praise
Thine eyes, and on thy forehead gaze.
Two hundred to adore each breast:
But thirty thousand to the rest.
An age at least to every part,
And the last age should show your heart.
For, lady, you deserve this state;
Nor would I love at lower rate.
   But at my back I always hear
Time's winged chariot hurrying near:
And yonder all before us lie
Deserts of vast eternity.
Thy beauty shall no more be found;

Nor, in thy marble vault, shall sound
My echoing song: then worms shall try
That long preserved virginity,
And your quaint honour turn to dust,
And into ashes all my lust.
The grave's a fine and private place,
But none I think do there embrace.
   Now therefore, while the youthful hue
Sits on thy skin like morning glew,
And while thy willing soul transpires
At every pore with instant fires,
Now let us sport us while we may;
And now, like amorous birds of prey,
Rather at once our time devour,
Than languish in his slow-chapt power.
Let us roll all our strength, and all
Our sweetness, up into one ball:
And tear our pleasures with rough strife
Thorough the iron gates of life.
Thus, though we cannot make our sun
Stand still, yet we will make him run.

ANDREW MARVELL

glew = glue, or maybe glow
chapt = chapped, or with a jaw

VENUS IN A LANDSCAPE, *Palma Vecchio*

One Day I Wrote Her Name

One day I wrote her name upon the strand,
    But came the waves, and washed it away.
    Again I wrote it with a second hand;
    But came the tide, and made my pains his prey.
'Vain man,' said she, 'that dost in vain assay
    A mortal thing so to immortalize;
    For I my self shall like to this decay,
    And eke my name be wiped out likewise.'
'Not so,' quoth I; 'let baser things devise
    To die in dust, but you shall live by fame:
    My verse your virtues rare shall eternize,
    And in the heavens write your glorious name,
Where, whenas death shall all the world subdue,
    Our love shall live, and later life renew.'

EDMUND SPENSER

THE VIRGIN OF CHANCELLOR ROLIN, *Jan van Eyck*

YOUNG WOMAN WITH A MIRROR, *Giovanni Bellini*

When Men Shall Find Thy Flower

When men shall find thy flower, thy glory pass,
   And thou with careful brow sitting alone,
Received had'st this message from thy glass,
   That tells the truth, and says that all is gone,
Fresh shalt thou see in me the wounds thou madest,
   Though spent thy flame, in me the heat remaining;
I that have loved thee thus before thou fadest,
   My faith shall wax, when thou art in thy waning.
The world shall find this miracle in me,
   That fire can burn when all the matter's spent;
Then what my faith hath been thyself shall see,
   And that thou wast unkind thou mayst repent.
     Thou mayst repent that thou hast scorned my tears,
     When winter snows upon thy sable hairs.

SAMUEL DANIEL

The Farewell to Worldly Love

Leave me, O love, which reachest but to dust,
And thou, my mind, aspire to higher things;
Grow rich in that which never taketh rust;
Whatever fades, but fading pleasure brings.
Draw in thy beams, and humble all thy might
To that sweet yoke where lasting freedoms be,
Which breaks the clouds, and opens forth the light
That doth both shine, and give us sight to see.
O take fast hold, let that light be thy guide
In this small course which birth draws out to death,
And think how ill becometh him to slide,
Who seeketh heaven, and comes of heavenly breath:
 Then farewell, world, thy uttermost I see;
 Eternal love, maintain thy life in me.
*Splendidis longum valedico nugis**

SIR PHILIP SIDNEY

*I say a long farewell to sumptuous nothings

'THE AMBASSADORS', *Hans Holbein the Younger*

That Time of Year

That time of year thou may'st in me behold
When yellow leaves, or none, or few do hang
Upon those boughs which shake against the cold,
Bare ruined choirs, where late the sweet birds sang.

In me thou seest the twilight of such day
As after sunset fadeth in the west,
Which by and by black night doth take away,
Death's second self, that seals up all in rest.

In me thou seest the glowing of such fire,
That on the ashes of his youth doth lie
As the deathbed whereon it must expire,
Consumed with that which it was nourished by:

This thou perceiv'st, which makes thy love more strong,
To love that well which thou must leave ere long.

WILLIAM SHAKESPEARE

PORTRAIT OF BATTISTA SFORZA, DUCHESS OF URBINO, *Piero della Francesca*

PORTRAIT OF FEDERICO DA MONTEFELTRO, DUKE OF URBINO, *Piero della Francesca*

# The Poets

Biographical information and text acknowledgements. Sources of texts are listed; spelling and punctuation have been modernized.

ANONYMOUS: The text of 'Greensleeves' appeared in a collection of ballads published in 1584, although it may well pre-date this. The text has been abridged: from *A Handful of Pleasant Delights (1584)*, ed. Hyder E. Rollins (Cambridge, Mass., 1924).

SAMUEL DANIEL (1563-1619) was educated at Magdalen Hall, Oxford. After travelling in Italy, he worked as a tutor before gaining favour at the court of James I with masques and plays. He eventually retired to Somerset. 'When Men Shall Find Thy Flower': from *Sonnets to Delia* in *The Works of the English Poets*, Vol. III, ed. Alexander Chalmers (London, 1810).

JOHN DONNE (1572-1631) was born in London and brought up as a Catholic. Although his religion debarred him from graduating, he was educated at Hart Hall, Oxford, and in Lincoln's Inn. He renounced his faith in the early 1590s. Donne became secretary to Sir Thomas Egerton, Lord Keeper of the Great Seal. A brilliant career was blighted by his secret marriage to Egerton's niece, Ann More, who died at the age of 33 after bearing twelve children, and he spent many years pursuing office. In 1621, he became Dean of St Paul's. 'The Good-Morrow', 'Song' and 'The Sun Rising': from *Poems* (London, 1650).

MICHAEL DRAYTON (1563-1631) was born in Warwickshire. He became a page to a wealthy family, but little is known about his life, which was probably spent in the households of patrons. He died comparatively poor, but was buried in Westminster Abbey, where his splendid monument was paid for by Lady Anne Clifford. He produced a great body of work, including odes, sonnets and satires, and religious and historical verse. 'Love in a Humour': from *Poems* (London, 1609).

JOHN FLETCHER (1579-1625) was born in Rye, Sussex. Educated at Benet (now Corpus Christi College), Cambridge, he collaborated with a number of playwrights, most notably Sir Francis Beaumont. Fletcher died of the plague. 'Tell Me, Dearest, What is Love?': from *English Songs*, ed. Edward Arber (London, New York and Toronto, 1908).

ROBERT GREENE (1558-92) was born in Norwich and educated at Cambridge. A prolific writer of plays, romances and pamphlets, he had a reputation as a drunkard, who abandoned his wife and children for the ladies of the taverns. A pamphlet after his early death (due, it was claimed, to an overdose of Rhenish wine and pickled herring) purported to express repentance for his wicked, but no doubt enjoyable, life. His often unremarkable dramas were redeemed by numerous examples of exquisite poetry. 'Sonnetto': from *Poems of Robert Greene and Christopher Marlowe*, ed. Robert Bell (London, 1856).

SIR FULKE GREVILLE, 1ST BARON BROOKE (1554-1628), was educated at Jesus College, Cambridge. A favourite of Elizabeth I, he wrote a *Life* of Sir Philip Sidney, which gives a vivid picture of contemporary court life. He also wrote over a hundred sonnets, didactic verse and two tragedies. He was murdered at the age of 74. 'The Nurse-Life Wheat' and 'The World, That All Contains': from *Cælica* in *The Works of Fulke Greville, Lord Brooke,* Vol. III, ed. Rev. Alexander B. Grosart (Lancashire, 1870).

ROBERT HERRICK (1591-1674) was the son of a goldsmith. After an apprenticeship in his father's trade, Herrick was educated at Cambridge, graduating in 1620, and took holy orders. He was deprived of his country living at Dean Prior in Devon for his royalist sympathies, but reinstated in 1660 and remained there for the rest of his life. A great lyric poet, his sophisticated verse explores sex, death and the transience of life, and reveals his interest in the frequently pagan folk rituals that the Puritans were anxious to suppress. 'Delight in Disorder' and 'To The Virgins, To Make Much of Time': from *Hesperides* (London, 1648).

THOMAS HEYWOOD (*c.* 1574-1641), actor, dramatist and poet, was educated at Cambridge and in 1598 joined Philip Henslowe's theatrical company, the Lord Admiral's Men. He collaborated in writing over two hundred plays, and also wrote poetry, pageants, tracts and treatises, and translations from Lucian, Erasmus and Ovid. His best and most well-known play is *A Woman Killed with Kindness* (1607). 'Pack, Clouds, Away': from *The Golden Treasury*, ed. F. T. Palgrave (London, 1884).

HENRY HOWARD, EARL OF SURREY, (*c.* 1517-47), married Frances Vere when still a boy and fought in France in the 1540s, before being executed for treasonable activities, on the flimsiest of evidence, when he was barely 30. With his contemporary Sir Thomas Wyatt, he is credited with the advancement of English poetry, in Surrey's case through the invention of the English form of the sonnet and his blank verse translations of Vergil's *Aeneid*. The plaintive lament 'O Happy Dames' is unusual in being written from a woman's point of view, and expresses what must have been a commonly felt anguish during this century of constant, perilous seagoing. 'O Happy Dames' and 'The Soote Season': from *Tottel's Miscellany*, ed. Edward Arber (London, 1870).

BEN JONSON (1572/3-1637) began work as a bricklayer, from where he went to Flanders on military service and won a single-combat contest with an enemy champion. After acting with a strolling company of players, he joined Philip Henslowe's companies, acting and writing. Ever quarrelsome, he killed a fellow actor in a duel, and was branded as a felon. His plays include *The Alchemist* and *Bartholomew Fair*, and he also collaborated with Inigo Jones on a series of masques. He was buried in Westminster Abbey. 'Song': from *Poetaster* (London, 1602).

THOMAS LODGE (1558-1625) was the son of Sir Thomas Lodge, lord mayor of London, and was educated at Trinity College, Oxford, and Lincoln's Inn. He went on buccaneering expeditions to the Canaries and South America, writing *Rosalynd* whilst tossed on the high seas. Shakespeare's *As You Like It* borrows heavily from this popular romance. Lodge wrote other romances, and sonnets, elegies and satirical poems, as well as translations from Seneca and *A Looking Glass for London and England* on which he collaborated with Robert Greene. 'Rosalynd's Madrigal': from *Rosalynd: Euphues Golden Legacie* (London, 1609).

RICHARD LOVELACE (1618-57/8) was imprisoned for his royalist sympathies, and saw his cause finally crushed by the execution of the king. Having expended his vast estates in Kent in Charles's cause, Lovelace died in great poverty. Despite his eventful life, Lovelace found the mental energy to write two dramas, now lost, and a body of often polished poetry: lyrics, odes, songs and sonnets. 'To Lucasta, Going to The Wars': from *Lucasta* (London, 1649).

The mysterious death of CHRISTOPHER MARLOWE (1564-93), stabbed in a tavern brawl, has led to speculation that this gifted playwright and poet was involved in the secret world of espionage and conspiracy that characterized Elizabethan politics. Whatever his political or religious affiliations, his drama was outstanding, introducing a revolutionary flexibility into the monolithic blank verse customarily used by playwrights, and paving the way for Shakespeare. 'Love in The Afternoon' is a translation from Ovid: from *The Works of Christopher Marlowe*, ed. Rev. Alexander Dyce (London, 1858); 'Love at First Sight' from *Hero and Leander*, ll. 167-176: from *Poems of Robert Greene and Christopher Marlowe*, ed. Robert Bell (London, 1856); 'The Passionate Shepherd to His Love': from *The Golden Treasury*, ed. F. T. Palgrave (London, 1884).

ANDREW MARVELL (1621-78) was educated at Cambridge and travelled in Europe before working as a tutor. Under Cromwell, he was appointed to John Milton's former post as Latin Secretary to the Council of State, and after the Protector's death, was elected MP for Hull. He seems to have continued his political involvements, travelling with embassies abroad and possibly engaging in espionage. His death is attributed to medical mismanagement. He was principally known as a satirist and political writer, and his lyric poems only achieved recognition in England in the twentieth century. 'To His Coy Mistress': from *Miscellaneous Poems* (London, 1681).

KATHERINE PHILIPS, the 'matchless Orinda', (1631/2-64) was married at the age of 16 to the parliamentarian James Philips, thirty-eight years her senior. Her poems began to be published in the 1650s. Despite her husband's political sympathies, she was herself a royalist and openly expressed her support after the Restoration of Charles II in 1660. Her translation of Corneille's tragedy *Pompey* was produced in Dublin in 1663 to great acclaim, and her collected poems were published apparently without authorization in 1664. She died of the smallpox. 'The Virgin': from *Poems* (London, 1667).

SIR WALTER RALEGH (1554?-1618) was one of the outstanding figures of the Elizabethan age. After a brief period at Oxford, he fought with the Huguenots in France, before embarking on his main career as traveller, explorer and colonizer, but he lost the Queen's favour by secretly marrying one of her ladies-in-waiting. With the fall of Essex, Ralegh's star rose again, but after the accession of James I he was tried for treason and incarcerated in the Tower for thirteen years, where he wrote his (incomplete) *History of the World*. An abortive trip in search of gold in 1616 led finally to his long-delayed execution. 'As You Came From The Holy Land': from *The Poems of Sir Walter Raleigh [sic] with those of Sir Henry Wotton*, ed. J. Hannah, DCL (London, 1875); 'Farewell, False Love': from *An English Garner*, ed. Edward Arber (London, 1903).

WILLIAM SHAKESPEARE (1564-1616) is known as England's greatest playwright, and was also an actor with management and ownership interests in the London theatre, and an esteemed poet. A self-made man, his output was prodigious, and his success in the theatre ensured material prosperity for his family. 'O Mistress Mine', 'That Time of Year' and 'To His Love': from *The Golden Treasury*, ed. F. T. Palgrave (London, 1884); 'The Expense of Spirit': from *Songs and Sonnets by William Shakespeare*, ed. F. T. Palgrave (London and Cambridge, 1865).

SIR PHILIP SIDNEY (1554-86) was born at Penshurst Place in Kent and educated at Oxford. He travelled in Europe, where he studied history and ethics, but on his return to England the expected political office did not arise until 1585 when he was appointed governor of Flushing. In the interim he concentrated on writing his prose romance, the *Arcadia*, the *Defence of Poetry*, and the sonnet sequence *Astrophel and Stella*, where Stella is believed to have been Penelope Devereux, who married Lord Rich two years before Sidney's own marriage to Frances Walsingham. Sidney had little time to enjoy his role in the Netherlands: he was wounded in an attack to prevent supplies reaching Zutphen, and died soon afterwards. His reputation as the perfect courtier and 'Renaissance man' has been exaggerated beyond his deserts, but his literary achievement is without question. 'Because I Breathe Not Love', 'My True Love Hath My Heart', 'The Farewell to Worldly Love' and 'Loving in Truth': from *The Countesse of Pembrokes Arcadia* (London, 1598).

ROBERT SIDNEY, EARL OF LEICESTER (1563-1626) was younger brother to Sir Philip Sidney. He too became governor of Flushing, remaining in the post for twenty years. 'The Sun is Set' appears in a manuscript volume dedicated to his sister, the Countess of Pembroke: from British Library MS Additional 58435 No. 120, f. 41r.

EDMUND SPENSER (c. 1552-99) was educated at Cambridge before obtaining a place with the Earl of Leicester. He was rewarded with Kilcolman Castle in the county of Cork for his work in the often ruthless 'settlement' of Ireland, but the castle was burned in a rebellion and Spenser died almost destitute. His most extensive work was *The Faerie Queene*, a vast allegorical poem which richly illuminates the Elizabethan age. 'The Bower of Bliss' from *The Faerie Queene*, Book 2, Canto xii, 'Coming to Kiss Her Lips', 'Like as a Huntsman' and 'One Day I Wrote Her Name': from *Complete Works of Edmund Spenser*, ed. R. Morris (London, 1879).

SIR JOHN SUCKLING (1609-41) came from an old Norfolk family and was educated at Cambridge. He travelled in Europe and then lived in great style at court. A royalist, he fled to France and is said to have committed suicide. His witty and elegant verse reflects his sparkling lifestyle as a polished courtier. 'Song': from *Fragmenta Aurea* (London, 1646).

EDWARD DE VERE, EARL OF OXFORD (1550-1604) was educated at Cambridge and made a prestigious marriage, but hopes of success at court were ruined by his quarrelsome nature. Greville records his famous dispute at a tennis match with Sir Philip Sidney, whom he addressed as 'puppy'. Few of his poems survive. 'A Renunciation': from *The Golden Treasury*, ed. F. T. Palgrave (London, 1884).

EDMUND WALLER (1606-87) was educated at Cambridge. He became a royalist and was banished for his role in a plot to seize London for Charles I, but achieved favour again with the Restoration. A favourite theme of his verse is praise of women. 'Song': from *Poems* (London, 1645).

Little is known about the playwright ROBERT WEAVER. His short moral play, *Lusty Juventus*, probably written in about 1550, supports reformist ideas by criticizing the superstitions of the papacy. 'In Youth is Pleasure': from *Lusty Juventus* (London, 1565?).

SIR HENRY WOTTON (1568-1639) was educated at Oxford and then travelled extensively in Europe. He was employed abroad in diplomacy and espionage, and made the famous comment: 'An Ambassador is an honest man, sent to lie abroad for the good of his country'. He eventually became provost of Eton. 'On His Mistress, The Queen of Bohemia': from *The Poems of Sir Walter Raleigh* [*sic*] *with those of Sir Henry Wotton*, ed. J. Hannah, DCL (London, 1875).

SIR THOMAS WYATT (1503-42) was educated at Cambridge and became a career diplomat in the service of Henry VIII. His reputed liaison with Anne Boleyn (probably the subject of 'Whoso List to Hunt') led to imprisonment in the Tower, but he then became ambassador to the Spanish court. With Cromwell's execution, Wyatt again fell from favour and he was charged with treason in 1541. Although released, he remained under a cloud and died soon afterwards of a fever. His poetry is characterized by variety of forms and metric experimentation, and by its direct speaking voice. 'They Flee From Me': from *Tottel's Miscellany*, ed. Edward Arber (London, 1870); 'Of The Pains and Sorrows Caused by Love': from *The Poetical Works of Sir Thomas Wyatt* (London, 1831); 'Whoso List to Hunt': from *The Poetical Works of Sir Thomas Wyatt and Henry Howard Earl of Surrey* (Boston, 1880).

Index

Acknowledgements

The editor would like to thank the following for their assistance: Sarah Blain, Courtauld Institute Galleries; Sue Daly, Fine Art Photographs; Sarah Goodbody, The Royal Collection; Francis Greenacre, Curator Fine Art, Bristol Museums and Art Gallery; Joanna Hartley and the staff of The Bridgeman Art Library; Alessandra Pinzani and the staff of SCALA Istituto Fotografico Editoriale, Florence; V & A Picture Library; Lavinia Wellicome, Curator, Woburn Abbey; Robin Harcourt Williams, Librarian & Archivist to the Marquess of Salisbury, Hatfield House; Vivien Bowler and Janet Ravenscroft of Little, Brown and Company.

The publisher would like to thank the following museums, galleries and individuals for supplying illustrations:

BRIDGEMAN ART LIBRARY: pp.12-13 Perseus freeing Andromeda, *Piero di Cosimo*, Uffizi Gallery, Florence (hereafter abr. to UG); p.22 Self-portrait with Gloves, *Albrecht Dürer*, Prado, Madrid; p.32 Portrait of a Lady, *Francesco Urbertini Verdi*, UG; p.45 Portrait of an Unknown Man, *Hans Memling*, UG; p.46 The Young Bacchus, *Caravaggio*, UG; p.64 The Three Ages of Man (detail), *Titian*, National Gallery of Scotland, Edinburgh; p.67 A Man and a Woman at a Casement, *Fra Filippo Lippi*, Metropolitan Museum of Art, New York; p.71 The Rape of Europa, *Francesco Albani*, UG; pp.74-5 The Andrians, *Titian*, Prado, Madrid; p.99 Portrait of a Lady, *Lucas Cranach the Elder*, Hermitage, Leningrad; p.108 Young Woman with a Mirror, *Giovanni Bellini*, Kunsthistorisches Museum, Vienna.

COURTAULD INSTITUTE GALLERIES, LONDON: p.105 Venus in a Landscape, *Palma Vecchio*.

COURTESY OF THE MARQUESS OF SALISBURY: p.29 The 'Rainbow' portrait of Queen Elizabeth I, *Isaac Oliver* (?).

GIRAUDON/BRIDGEMAN ART LIBRARY: p.25 Gabrielle d'Estrées and her sister, the Duchess of Villars, *School of Fontainebleau*, Louvre, Paris; p.60 The Moneylender and his Wife, *Quentin Massys*, Louvre, Paris; p.77 Diana the Hunter, *Orazio Gentileschi*, Musée des Beaux-Art, Nantes; p.107 The Virgin of Chancellor Rolin, *Jan van Eyck*, Louvre, Paris.

NATIONAL GALLERY: p.14 Mercury instructing Cupid before Venus, *Correggio*; p.21 An Allegory with Venus and Cupid, *Agnolo Bronzino*; p.26 'The Arnolfini Marriage', *Jan van Eyck*; p.39 Cupid complaining to Venus, *Lucas Cranach the Elder*; p.41 Portrait of a Young Man, *Moretto da Brescia*; p.72 Venus and Mars, *Botticelli*; p.78 A Blonde Woman, *Palma Vecchio*; p.81 Bacchus and Ariadne, *Titian*; p.90 Portrait of a Lady, *Lorenzo Lotto*; p.97 and cover The Toilet of Venus, *Diego Velázquez*; p.103 Portrait of a Lady in Yellow, *Alesso Baldovinetti*; p.111 'The Ambassadors', *Hans Holbein the Younger*.

PHOTO SCALA, FLORENCE: pp.2-3 Sacred and Profane Love, *Titian*, Borghese Gallery, Rome; p.17 Leda, (after) *Leonardo da Vinci*, Borghese Gallery, Rome; p.18 Flora, *Carlo Cignani*, Estense Gallery, Modena; p.31 Pastoral Concert, *Titian*, Louvre, Paris; pp.34-5 Primavera (detail), *Botticelli*, UG; p.42 The Month of April (detail), *Francesco del Cossa*, Schifanoia Palace, Ferrara; p.49 The Rape of Proserpine, *Niccolò dell'Abate*, Louvre, Paris; p.51 Portrait of a Cavalier, *Vittore Carpaccio*, Thyssen Collection; p.52 Ariadne abandoned, *Gerolamo del Pacchia*, Chigi Saracini Collection, Siena; pp.54-5 The Meeting of St Ursula with her Betrothed (detail), *Vittore Carpaccio*, Accademia Gallery, Venice; p.57 The Venus of Urbino, *Titian*, UG; p.59 The Contest between Marsyas and Apollo, *Perugino*, Louvre, Paris; p.63 The Meeting of Frederick III and Eleanor of Aragon (detail), *Bernardino Betti, Il Pinturicchio*, Duomo, Siena; p.68 The Hunt of Charles V (detail), *Lucas Cranach the Elder*, Prado, Madrid; p.82 The Magdalene, *Caravaggio*, Doria Pamphili Gallery, Rome; p.85 The Pearl Fishers, *Alessandro Allori*, Palazzo Vecchio, Florence; p.86 Susanna at her Bath, *Palma il Giovane*, Chigi Saracini Collection, Siena; p.89 Servants with a Horse and Dogs (detail), *Andrea Mantegna*, Palazzo Ducale, Mantova; p.93 Adam and Eve, *Lucas Cranach the Elder*, UG; pp.94-5 The Birth of Venus, *Botticelli*, UG; p.100 Venus and Mars, *Paolo Veronese*, Sabauda Gallery, Turin; p.113 Portrait of Battista Sforza, Duchess of Urbino and Portrait of Federico da Montefeltro, Duke of Urbino, *Piero della Francesca*, UG.

ROYAL COLLECTION, ST. JAMES'S PALACE: © H.M. THE QUEEN: p.36 Portrait of a Young Man, *Isaac Oliver*.

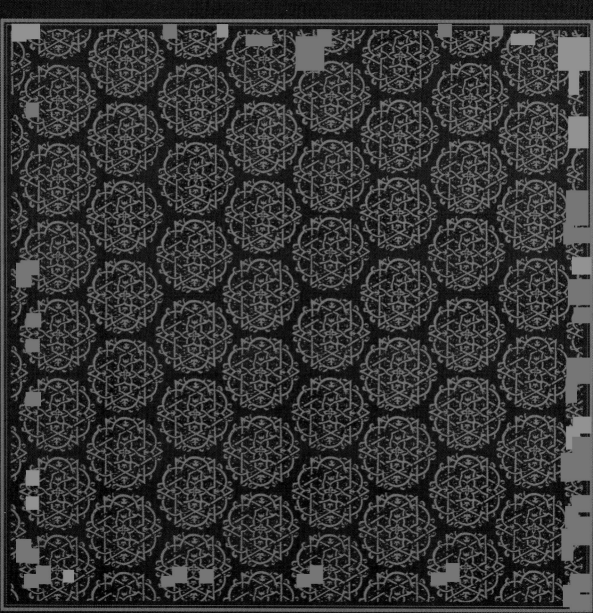